Mirror Mirror
IN THE
Trash

To Carrie + Vicky —
2 beautiful women that
I love! Thanks
for your friendship
+ support!
Love,
Bobbie

Mirror Mirror IN THE Trash

Thoughts on Valuing Your Inner Beauty

BOBBIE D'ADDARIO

Knowlton Avenue Press

Mirror Mirror in the Trash: Thoughts on Valuing Your Inner Beauty
Published by Knowlton Avenue Press
Aurora, CO.

Publisher's Cataloging-in-Publication data

Names: D'Addario, Bobbie, author.
Title: Mirror, mirror in the trash : thoughts on valuing your inner beauty / Bobbie D'Addario.
Description: Aurora [Colorado] : Knowlton Avenue Press, 2019. First original paperback edition. Also available as an ebook.
Identifiers: ISBN 978-1-7328796-0-7
Subjects: LCSH: Self-esteem in women—Anecdotes. | Self-acceptance. | Women—Psychology—Anecdotes.
BISAC: BODY, MIND & SPIRIT / Inspiration & Personal Growth
Classification: LCC BF575.S37 2019 | DDC 158.1–dc22

Cover by Victoria Wolf and Interior design by Andrea Costantine

QUANTITY PURCHASES: Schools, companies, professional groups, clubs, and other organizations may qualify for special terms when ordering quantities of this title. For information, email info@KnowltonAvenuePress.com.

To Bob, who thinks I'm beautiful, just as I am...
and to my children, Kelsey and Nick,
who taught me what being "beautiful" is all about!

Table of Contents

Preface

I want to thank the close to one hundred teen girls and women that contributed their thoughts and stories with me to make this book a reality. I have been teaching classes on body image and self-esteem to teenage girls and women for the past twenty years. The classes were birthed from a need I witnessed almost daily in my work as a youth director at a United Methodist Church beginning in 1996. At that time, there was not much written about self-esteem and body image that was useful for my work. After an extensive search, I ended up writing my own curriculum. Building young girls and women up became a part of my daily routine with the idea of loving oneself throughout one's life at the forefront. I should not have been surprised this was such a major talking point with teenage girls. I had been struggling with body image and self-esteem issues for as long as I could remember.

The more I taught the class, the more I realized that this class would never be a one-shot deal. The girls that took the class loved it and kept wanting more. The women that I shared it with desired more as well. I came to realize that no matter how old we are, there is always a need to be reminded of our beauty and our worth. For those of us fortunate to be surrounded by people who truly love us for who we are, it is a definite advantage but surely not a cure-all.

If there is one thing that I've learned, it is that we all want to be beautiful. Some of us are wise enough to remember that inner beauty is more important than our outward appearance. Some might believe that people just use that expression to make them feel better when they are having an "ugly" day. I think it's safe to say that women of all ages want to feel beautiful on the inside and outside as well.

I remember when my daughter went through a stage of constantly looking in the mirror. It drove me a bit crazy, but I understood it. I prayed that she would see her beauty the way I did.

I have shared my "Body and Soul" curriculum with hundreds of women and girls, and I am always amazed at how much I continue to learn. I am thankful for those conversations, and I'm looking forward to sharing that insight with you.

Whether you have purchased this book for you or for someone you love, keep in mind that this is a journey that we are all on at one time or another. I am blessed to feel that I am a beautiful child of God. Others that read this book may have other ideas about religion, inner peace or spirituality.

I offer this only as a way to say that most of us are moved by something. For many, it is a higher power, nature, music, or relationships. Whatever that might be for you as a reader, I hope that you will take time as you go through this book to meditate, listen and to pay attention. Being present to others is a rare gift these days and paying attention to our own needs can be rare as well.

For the past thirty-three years, I have been married to a wonderful man who has loved me from 130 pounds to 230 pounds and everywhere in between. Even at my heaviest weight, he has told me I am beautiful. I always knew, however, that I was the one that had to believe it. Over the years I have had moments of incredible confidence, as well as moments when I hated everything about the way I looked. I have had more love for my personality and ability to make friends than I have ever had for my appearance. I am thankful that most days I like who I am, and who I am as a person in relationships with others. No matter how much time goes by, though, I realize that self-esteem and a healthy body image will be a work in progress. I also believe that this is true for many women I know.

More often than not, people have trouble loving themselves the way that, I believe, God created them to be. I have the most experience with teenage girls and women, so the bulk of the information in this book is about those two demographics.

I don't believe that this insecurity gives us an excuse not to care for ourselves by eating healthy, exercising, and making good choices. I know that good intentions are not always enough. The frustration and lack of motivation that can accompany depression or physical disabilities are completely understandable. I have learned that understanding where some of the negative self-talk comes from can help us to control our actions a bit more. I also wholeheartedly believe that we are all incredibly unique and special. Many of us will spend a lifetime looking for something unique about ourselves, and we might have a difficult time believing that we are extraordinary. Some people are lucky enough to figure it out at a young age, and I hope that they treasure that awareness.

This book is designed to help women of all ages have the important and deep conversations that are essential for growth. It is a vehicle to promote sharing and an opportunity to think about what we love and treasure about others and ourselves. It is a tool to be used in book groups, workshops, retreats, and classes. It can also be used individually as a journal for self-discovery.

Most importantly, I hope this book inspires women and girls to share their stories.... Their moments of joy and celebration of who they are. Hopefully, it is also an opportunity for women to see that the insecurity and self-doubt that they struggle with is more common than any of us would ever believe. I am always amazed that after I share my stories of insecurity, anxiety, and depression that women say to me, "I thought you had it all together!"

The book begins with girls between the ages of ten to fourteen and ends with women in the later years of their lives. I tried to cover the common questions that we think about often but don't talk about nearly enough. My hope and prayer is that in some of the sharing you will have an "AHA" moment as one of my favorite pastors would call it (miss you, Reverend Marti) and that in that moment something will ring so true that you cannot help but be challenged or changed by it. For some of you, there may be many of those moments, and if so, I hope that this book will be shared among friends, colleagues, sisters, and loved ones.

On a regular basis, I continue to remind myself to practice self-care. For me, the insecurities sometimes run so deep that I still might struggle, especially when it comes to managing my weight. The more that I share my thoughts with other women, the more I realize we all have at least one weak spot that challenges us. The most influential role models in my life have been spiritual leaders, teachers, family, and friends.... People that inspire and love me in ways that I never imagined. I pray that whoever studies this book finds a way to connect to God (or some higher power) and others, but most of all that you find a way to love yourself. For all of us, I wish blessings on the journey.

*Answers to questions were kept as they were submitted without grammatical corrections.

*Answers from those listed as "anonymous" are from multiple people.

ONE

From Toys to Boys

"Beauty is in the eye of the beholder and it may be
necessary from time to time to give a stupid or
misinformed beholder a black eye."
— Miss Piggy

Recently I heard that girls in elementary school are already being diagnosed with eating disorders and other maladies that stem from a lack of self-esteem. I think back to what I cared about most when I was an eight-year-old girl and all that comes to mind are Barbie dolls, playing outside with friends, and doing well in school. I don't remember thinking much about what I looked like at the time. I know that I liked to hang out with my friends and laugh a lot.

I know that by middle school, my thoughts about myself changed dramatically. I cared far too much about what I looked like in those years. The mirror became too important. Thankfully, those thoughts did not begin at such a young age as eight. It saddens me to think that this burden now starts so early because I know that it can become a lifelong battle. For this younger age group, I asked questions that were more general in nature. I have used the answers that I thought most fitting for this book. My hope is that as you get to the chapters that are directed toward older girls and women, you will have had a chance to think back to when you were a child and what some of your hopes and dreams were at that age.

I don't know many women that would say that the best time of their life was the end of grade school and the beginning of middle school. It is an incredibly awkward age. Your body is changing in ways that you barely understand. Even the girls that you consider to be your closest friends are not always nice.

I was just completing seventh grade when my parents told us that we were moving. We were leaving a relatively large suburb of Buffalo, New York, Kenmore, to move to the small town of Wilson, New York (about thirty-five miles away). I was devastated. I had been in the same house since I was three years old, and I loved my life.

I have wonderful memories of growing up in Kenmore with lots of friends to play ditch and kickball with. On the rainy days, we would start Monopoly games that lasted for days, left set up on the coffee table. I had also started what we called "junior high" back then and had successfully transitioned well to that with many girlfriends and my first boyfriend. Not that the boyfriend was anything serious, but it had given me the confidence to make friends with people that I might have otherwise thought "too popular" for me.

Thinking back to this age reminds me that many of the girls that I have worked with over the years fall prey to these very same thoughts. The idea that a boy can make you fit in better, the thought that the popular group will mean happiness in school, or that if you have the right clothes and haircut, all will be right with your world. Like many women, it saddens me to see young girls have a dependence on boys or the "right stuff" to build up their self-esteem.

I had always made friends easily, but moving in the summer was a real challenge. The house in Kenmore had been a very safe place for me, and I learned to treasure safe places more as I aged.

The first friend I met in our new town was already drinking alcohol and participating in activities that I had never considered at that age. When I tried to disengage from the friendship, I was bullied for almost two full school years. This included me being beaten up in front of a crowd of laughing kids and regularly being shoved into the lockers at school. I was fortunate to make friends easily still, and the girl that was so mean had a bad enough reputation to warrant empathy and understanding from others. I found my secure place in the music and theater programs at school and a wonderful youth group at a United Methodist Church.

With the love of great friends and amazing youth sponsors, (thank you John and Gary Stevens) I was able to grow into the person that God had created me to be. But we all know that these middle school years can change the course of a life. This is especially true if there is any kind of physical or sexual abuse, emotional neglect, verbal abuse, or trauma. We all have baggage that we carry with us from our families of origin, and many of our self-esteem issues begin at this age.

In my job as a social worker, and then a youth pastor for many years, I was blessed to work with extraordinary young girls. I now have the privilege to know them, as they became incredible young adults and beautiful, successful women.

I have chosen many topics for this book that were discussed in "Body and Soul" retreats and classes. I have been inspired by the women and teenage girls that have shared their stories and answers with me. Some contributors to this book chose to share anonymously, and many were willing to share their stories more publicly. These are the questions and answers from the youngest group surveyed.

10–14 YEARS OLD

What do you appreciate the most about your life?

Maddie, 13: I appreciate all the people in my life that make it so special because without my friends and family my life would most definitely not be the same and that makes life itself special in my opinion. I appreciate the memories I have, both good and bad, that define who I am. I like that I am confident in myself and that I'd much rather be who I really am rather than who people want or expect me to be.

Emily: I appreciate my friends and all of my family.

Sarah: I have a really awesome life without anything awful ever happening. But I guess what I appreciate most is my friends and family who make me laugh every day and support me through everything!

Anonymous: I appreciate my family and friends. I also appreciate lots of forms of art such as film and writing, since they are perhaps my greatest passions. I love and respect anyone who works in the art department, especially film since they put so much time and effort into their creations.

Caitlin, 14: I appreciate being able to spend time with those I love, whether they be friends or family. I enjoy their company.

Discussion Questions for All Ages:

Clearly, at ages 10–14, friends and family are very high on the list. On a scale of one to ten (one being the most important), where would you put the people that you are closest to?

1. _____
2. _____
3. _____
4. _____
5. _____
6. _____
7. _____
8. _____
9. _____
10. _____

Do you remember what you were most grateful for at this age? Has that changed?

_____

_____

_____

_____

_____

_____

_____

How does your delegation of time compare to what you appreciate and value the most?

_____

_____

_____

_____

_____

Please use this space to make a list of ten things that you are most grateful for:

1. _____

2. _____

3. _____

4. _____

5. _____

6. _____

7. _____

8. _____

9. _____

10. _____

What do you imagine you will be like at thirty?

Maddie, 13: When I'm thirty, I see myself having kids and being a role model for them. I see myself having a job and a family that I love and trust. I see myself still being healthy and confident and I also see having some of the same friends that I have grown close to over the years. I imagine that I will have a life that I am happy to live knowing that I've faced those difficult challenges head on. At thirty, I don't want to regret the choices I've made up until then, I want to know that there was a reason for making them even if I didn't see it at the time.

Emily: By that time I want to be senator of Pennsylvania so that I can become president of the United States later on in life.

Sarah: I hope I will have a family but I will still be really modern! I imagine I will be sort of similar to how I am now but I probably will be more serious and not as carefree in the future. (Sorry I know that answer is vague. Truth is I have no idea what I will be like in 30 years).

Anonymous: When I am 30 I imagine myself as probably just on the brink of settling down and possibly getting married. I am not planning on having kids while I am in my 20s. I hope that by that time I will be established enough so I will have a home and a secure job where I get to do something that I enjoy.

Caitlin, 14: I imagine to have a career and a family of my own. I hope to be living comfortably and enjoying my life!

Discussion Questions for All Ages:

Did some of the answers from this chapter remind you of your hopes at that age?

_____

_____

_____

_____

_____

_____

_____

_____

_____

Do you believe that you have accomplished your most important goals?

_____

_____

_____

_____

_____

_____

Did anything get in the way of you pursuing your goals and if so, how did you redirect yourself?

_____

_____

_____

_____

_____

_____

_____

_____

_____

Picture yourself at age thirty. Either draw a picture of what you think you might look like or what you did look like:

What do you like most about the way you look?

Maddie, 13: I like that my look is more natural. I like the way I look without makeup and I like that I can feel confident about the way I look even if it is casual and not dressed up. I also like how even though I'm not stick-skinny, I'm not overweight and I like that my size doesn't matter to me as long as I feel confident and know that I'm healthy.

Emily: The thing that I like most about how I look is my red hair.

Sarah: My hair. It's naturally curly and I used to hate it but now I really love it.

Anonymous: I like my eyes (when they are not swelling up) as well as my form and height. I do not feel like I am overweight and my height (5 foot) is perfect since I am tall enough to ride roller coasters but I'm not constantly banging my head on things.

Caitlin, 14: I love my eyes! They are green with gold in the middle and navy around the outside. I can gaze at them for hours.

Discussion Questions for All Ages:

Do you believe it is easier to love your appearance when you are younger?

_____

_____

_____

_____

_____

What do you value the most about your appearance as you age?

_____

_____

_____

_____

_____

Have you struggled with one or two appearance frustrations, and if so, how have you dealt with that frustration?

_____

_____

_____

_____

_____

Write a poem about your joys or frustrations (For those of you that have not done much writing, there is no right or wrong way to do this. Words do not have to rhyme, just be written from your heart):

_____

_____

_____

_____

_____

_____

_____

_____

What do you like most about the way you feel?

_____

_____

_____

_____

Maddie, 13: I like that when I feel, I know that I am human, and I have emotions and that that's okay. I like knowing that I am expressing myself through how I feel, even if it's in private. I like being able to know that life isn't just perfection, it comes with sorrow and depressing times and that it's okay to not always be the happy person that people want to see. But I also like that I can be happy, even in difficult times if I find it somewhere deep inside. I like knowing that feeling is a part of being human.

Caitlin, 14: I like that I feel happy quite often. It doesn't take much to get me smiling!

Emily: I like most that after I do something that I enjoy I feel really enthusiastic.

Sarah: My confidence. I was so insecure last year in 7th grade and 6th grade. I have grown more confident and it has changed my life. I am happier and I can't imagine ever wanting to be the insecure person I was.

Anonymous: I like that I am happy most of the time, and that I can usually just go with what is thrown at me. I do have problems with stress, and at times can be depressed, but for the most part I have a lot of energy.

Discussion Questions for All Ages:

What do you like or miss the most about how you feel or felt at this age?

_____

_____

_____

_____

_____

_____

_____

Has your confidence level increased as you have aged, why or why not?

_____

_____

_____

_____

_____

What are the moments in your life that you remember with the most emotion?

_____

_____

_____

_____

_____

Try writing an emotion poem here, an example might be that you feel most calm when, or happiest when...):

_____

_____

_____

_____

_____

_____

_____

_____

_____

_____

_____

_____

_____

_____

_____

_____

_____

_____

TWO

Sixteen, Going on Seventeen ...

"Think of all the beauty still left around you and be happy."
— Anne Frank (1929–1945), *Diary of a Young Girl*, 1952

We may remember our high school years with nostalgic smiles or quiet disdain. Some women found those years to be filled with friendship, laughter, and possibilities. Others may have wanted this time of life to be over quickly in order to move on to the next chapter. I was one of the lucky ones. I went to one high school through tenth grade and then moved before my junior year. My last two years of high school were in a large high school with a graduating class of close to 800 students, a class size easy to get lost in if one does not find their niche.

The beginning of my junior year was a bit difficult, as most people had already formed their tight-knit group of friends. I was fortunate to find my place in the theater and choir and later student government, I was grateful for that.

Part of the reason making friends came easily to me was that I was never really one to stay home with family. My mom worked long hours as a labor and delivery nurse, my dad worked off and on, but when he was home, he kept to himself at home with his painting and hobbies. I was the third of four kids, middle of the girls, and often felt I was the one left out. Friends became my family substitute at a young age. I had learned to attach myself to friends that had loud, noisy families since my home life was rather quiet.

My parents had come over from England when my oldest sister was three and the rest of us were born in America. Our family was reserved compared to most American families that I knew. I developed a love for reading and writing at a young age, but when I was around others, I blossomed.

I remember being the kid on the block to organize group games and storytelling. I knew just about everyone on the block growing up, and I knew where to go for the best snacks and the most fun. When I was old enough to babysit, I was the teenager that for fifty cents an hour would not only watch the four children but also play games with them and clean the house too. It was not uncommon for me to lead a pack of kids on a three-mile walk to the Buffalo Zoo.

During the three years of middle school in a very small town, I learned so much about the importance of community. I was there for eighth, ninth, and tenth grades but my parents never acclimated to small-town life. They found people to be very unfriendly to newcomers. I was fortunate to find a youth group and youth sponsors that shaped my faith and my life in ways that I never expected. It was during those years that I learned that God was a huge part of my life because although I had always believed in God, I began to feel God at work in my life. I think that the greatest blessing in my life at this time was a group of friends that would have done anything for each other. Middle school girls can be a really tough bunch, but I was blessed with friends who built each other up, kept quiet about each other's secrets, and shared all that they had.

The drawback to my middle school years was that I began to notice all of the ways that I felt inferior to other girls. My mother worked hard as a nurse, but my dad was an artist at heart and often out of work, so we lived on a very strict budget. Fashionable clothes were not in any way a priority. My older sister was seven years ahead of me. She was short and as skinny as a rail, very much like the British model Twiggy who was all over magazine covers in the late sixties and early seventies. I was given hand me down clothes that had been hers, but I was five inches taller and with that came an additional twenty pounds.

I remember wishing that I attended a school that had a uniform, just so that there would not be so much pressure to look a certain way. I began babysitting and doing a paper route just so that I could buy clothes that were more in style with what the other girls were wearing. I look back now and realize that at sixteen I was five foot eight inches tall, weighed in at about 120 pounds and began to think I was fat.

I had friends that tried to reassure me that I was not fat, that I was pretty and worrying needlessly. Even with their kind words, I never felt that I quite measured up. I was a good student, popular in school, had a nice singing voice and parts in most school musicals and plays, but still lacked the confidence that I should have had. I look back to this time in my life and feel such regret that I did not appreciate my health, beauty, gifts, and talents. It is a lesson that I continue to be reminded of as I age.

Like most girls that age who are unsure of themselves, I found confidence in getting attention from boys. I started sexual experimentation too young, and I am amazed to this day that I held on to my virginity until I had been dating my husband for several months into our college life. I sensed a power that girls had over boys at a young age, but didn't realize the damage that I was doing to my self-esteem by making out and fooling around with too many boys. Moving before my junior year became a blessing as I was dangerously close to crossing some lines with a boy that I really believed I loved with all of my heart. He was a boy in my youth group, whose sister was my very good friend, a recipe for disaster in itself. Looking back now I realize how drawn I was to the whole family. They were fun and fun loving, always on the go and they were loud. Having always felt a bit too active and loud in the home I came from, I longed for that kind of joyful atmosphere.

Looking back now on that time in my life. I know that girls will do all kinds of things that they may not be comfortable with to be accepted and admired. I am not sure we ever realize it at the time, but it is fairly common with most teenage girls to want the attention of a boy, any boy....

After years of working with middle school and senior high youth, I have now seen it from the other side. I watch these dramas play out again and again before my eyes. The cat and mouse, the attention seekers, the shy girls, the difference a little bit of self-love and confidence can make. I think this is part of what inspired me to begin the Body and Soul classes in the first place. For many girls starting high school, a close group of friends, and adults that they can talk openly with can make a huge difference.

As a youth pastor, I was able to see how involving young people in community service became a great way to keep them away from the mirror. When you are working with those much less fortunate, hair and makeup fall far down on the list of priorities.

I would encourage any young person to consider getting involved in service to others when life is not seeming as good as it can be. I have seen this change hearts and, in turn, change lives! Next are the questions and answers from girls in this age group.

15–18 YEAR OLD GIRLS

What have been your greatest achievements and your greatest challenges so far?

Olivia, 18: I have been challenged with my parents' divorce and financial struggles living with two single parents, but I have overcome these hardships but expressing myself through school activities. I was the senior drum major of my high school marching band, the Key Club president and awarded the title of a Daniel's scholar.

Anonymous: Greatest challenge—depression and the incredible strain it puts on my relationships with other people. Greatest achievements are finally getting help with depression and probably also winning some sweet scholarship awards.

Hayli, 15: My greatest achievements are learning how to play the flute, gaining more confidence in myself. My greatest challenges have been balancing everything and finding time to hang out with my friends.

Discussion Questions for All Ages:

High school can be difficult at times and joyful as well. What do you remember most about this time?

_____

_____

_____

_____

_____

_____

_____

_____

_____

_____

_____

_____

_____

How might your achievements motivate you to go out on a limb?

_____

_____

_____

_____

_____

_____

_____

_____

_____

_____

Can you identify with "fitting in" or "feeling left out?" If so, how has this changed over the years?

_____

_____

_____

_____

_____

I am most motivated when... Things that make me struggle are... (Write a conversation poem or thoughts)

_____

_____

_____

_____

_____

What is the quality that you love the most about yourself?

Olivia, 18: I love my work ethic and my willingness to try new things even if that does mean I am putting myself out on the line.

Anonymous: I'm incredibly compassionate. Sometimes to a painful degree. If there is such a thing as caring too much, I do it.

Hayli, 15: The quality that I love the most about myself is my big brown eyes and my smile.

Discussion Questions for All Ages:

What is the easiest thing to love about you?

_____

_____

_____

_____

_____

When are the times that you have felt unlovable?

_____

_____

_____

_____

Things that make me feel loved:

_____

_____

_____

_____

_____

What is the most meaningful relationship in your life right now?

Olivia, 18: My most meaningful relationship in my life right now is with my mom and dad. They have been very supportive in the transition from high school to college, as well as being the biggest "fanners" of my flame.

Anonymous: My friend at work. He is one of the most charismatic, narcissistic individuals I know and he tells me almost every day how great I am. Most days I really need to hear that and somehow his narcissism makes it more poignant. Narcissists don't just throw around compliments to other people, Willy-Nilly.

Hayli, 15: The most meaningful relationship in my life right now would be the relationship between me and my mom.

Discussion Questions for All Ages:

What makes a relationship meaningful for you?

_____

_____

_____

_____

_____

_____

How do you nurture your relationships?

_____

_____

_____

_____

_____

A relationship is... (Thoughts or poem)

_____

_____

_____

_____

_____

_____

_____

_____

THREE

Coming Into My Own

"Everything has its beauty but not everyone sees it."
— Confucius (551 BC–479 BC)

Many of us remember our high school days fondly. It was a time to be a little crazy, test the waters and be incredibly busy (without the exhaustion part). For teenage girls today, there is more pressure than ever to be thin, have perfect skin, nails, clothes, and many more layers of vanity. We are bombarded with perfect images in magazines, movies, and television that portray unattainable pictures.

I love when the girls I work with go out of their comfort zone, break the rules, and love themselves for who they are. I have been on numerous mission trips where the girls couldn't care less about makeup or having their hair look nice. It was always about service and getting out of our own way.

In September of 2014, I was blessed to go with World Vision to Ecuador. We visited villages where I saw poverty that I had only previously witnessed on videos. The people were incredibly joyful and therefore, exceptionally beautiful. I never saw a mirror anywhere.

It is said that we are at our most beautiful when we are talking about something that we feel passionate about. I know this is true for me. I also believe that we are our best selves when we let go of our own worries and fears and focus on what we can do for others. I have found that teenage girls who learn this lesson at an early age, grow into breathtaking women.

For many girls in high school, there may not be an opportunity to have this kind of mission or volunteer experience. If you are not religious or prefer not to be involved in organized religion, I strongly urge you to find a place to volunteer. Showing compassion for others can ease tension, anxiety, and feelings of depression. I have witnessed this time and time again during my years of youth ministry.

Boys that are involved in these same philanthropic activities seem to have a greater sense of self and are likely to be loving, caring, young men. There are many things that we can teach our children at home, but volunteer work offers reinforcement that is extremely powerful.

As I read the answers to the questions below, it was apparent to me that this age group is "others" centered and often sees the larger picture better than many adults do. Some may say that it is because they are young and inexperienced, or because they have not tried and failed too many times. I believe that young people in this age group have a greater understanding about what is happening in the world and are concerned with how they can make a difference. They are not easily dissuaded from causes that they are passionate about. We can learn great things from this age group.

POST HIGH SCHOOL
What is the greatest life lesson you have learned so far?

Abby, 18: The greatest life lesson I have learned so far is that there is more to the world than what I am focused on. There is always going to be someone who is in a worse situation than I am, so I try to take the time to pray and to adjust my perspective every time I get overwhelmed with what is going on with my life.

Emily, 19: The greatest lesson in life I have learned so far is to pursue the life I want for myself and to always be kind.

Lex: To stay true to who you are without letting others define you.

Abi, 18: Self-love and self-trust. Sometimes I still struggle with these, but I have found that the more I trust myself, and the more I truly love myself and accept myself for who I am and who I want to be, that I open myself up to more opportunities and relationships than if I was full of doubt and self-hatred.

Tori, 19: The greatest life lesson I have learned so far is that everyone deserves to be loved. No one should ever be judged for who they are, their sexual orientation, how they identify etc.

Hannah, 18: Never stop trying, you can't give up on anything or anyone. No matter how hard things get giving up is never an option.

MacKenzie, 21: The greatest life lesson I have learned so far is that finding who you are in your own way is the most valuable thing you can do for yourself.

Discussion Questions for All Ages:

Does it seem that the older you get, the more you learn?

_____

_____

_____

_____

_____

Post high school years can be incredibly challenging and frightening sometimes, what is your greatest fear right now?

_____

_____

_____

_____

_____

Write a poem or some thoughts about what fear is:

_____

_____

_____

_____

_____

_____

What is the most exciting part of your life right now?

Abby, 18: I am most excited about how I am getting to decide who I am right now. I am experiencing new things, meeting new people with new perspectives and learning from them. I am learning for myself what I believe about God, about what is right and wrong, and about how to respond to different people and situations.

Emily, 19: I'm just finishing my first year of college and I'm just excited to continue with school and then go on to have the career I've always dreamed of. I am very happy right now. I'm successful in school, I have amazing friends, a fantastic job, and I'm just excited to alive, healthy, and happy!

Lex: Getting ready to end the high school chapter and begin to be on my own in college.

Abi, 18: The most exciting part of my life right now is testing limits-especially my own. This goes for academic challenges, my social life, and the depths of my own personality. I feel like I am at an age where I am really just starting to discover myself and the world around me and it's an adventure.

Anonymous, 19: Being in college and thinking about all the different opportunities that lay ahead. I think about my goals right now and wonder what might be different in five, ten, or fifteen years, and that's both scary and really exciting!

Tori, 19: The most exciting part in my life currently is getting the opportunity to teach something I love.

Hannah, 18: Being able to start college and a new life. Being on my own and away from my parents.

MacKenzie, 21: The most exciting thing in my life right now is I just moved into my very first apartment!

Discussion Questions for All Ages:

What is the most exciting part of your life right now?

_____

_____

_____

_____

_____

If you are having trouble getting excited about anything, why do you think that is?

_____

_____

_____

_____

What is testing you currently?

_____

_____

_____

_____

What is your biggest fear or worry?

Anonymous, 19: Not making meaningful relationships, or not maintaining the ones I do make (for instance, when I leave college).

Abby, 18: Right now, my biggest fears and worries seem to be pretty trivial, because I am in a pretty good place with myself, but I worry about school and doing well, and being sucked into petty drama and gossiping that could end up hurting someone. I always try to be the person who gives the benefit of the doubt and who doesn't assume things, but when I am surrounded by it all the time, it is hard to avoid.

Emily, 19: I am worried that I won't be successful. I am scared that I will get out of college and I won't be able to find a job in my career field and that I'll be stuck living with my parents for the rest of my life.

Lex: Not being successful in my career field

Abi, 18: Not reaching my fullest potential or overreaching my limits. I like to take on tasks like challenges and sometimes end up with what most would say is too much on my plate. It scares me to think of how taking all this now will impact my future and if I was really ever ready to take on half the challenges I have.

Tori, 19: My biggest fear is that I won't ever love myself enough for someone else to love me.

Hannah, 18: I'm afraid that I'm going to lose touch with people and scared of everything changing.

MacKenzie, 21: My biggest fear is that I am not doing everything that I want to do while I am at this age.

Discussion Questions for All Ages:

What is your greatest fear or worry in your life right now?

_____

_____

_____

_____

_____

_____

_____

_____

_____

How do you handle fear and worry?

_____

_____

_____

_____

_____

_____

_____

_____

Write about what you believe success is:

_____

_____

_____

_____

_____

_____

_____

_____

_____

_____

What are your dreams for the future?

_____

_____

_____

_____

_____

_____

_____

_____

_____

_____

_____

Abby, 18: In the future I hope to have a job that I enjoy and is ideally doing something to better the world, and a family.

Emily, 19: I hope to be a non-profit manager in an organization like World Vision. I want to save people's lives by feeding them and providing things for them.

Lex: To open my own studio and love to teach kids to express themselves through dance.

Abi, 18: I want to never stop growing as a person. I want to graduate college with high honors and go on to grad school for a double masters. I have dreams of traveling the world and then settling down with the one I love all the while making a difference in this world.

Anonymous, 19: Being able to look back and be proud of what I have accomplished. I want to go into education, and make a difference there by teaching young minds. But I would also love to keep learning--researching, post-graduate education, something like that. I have big dreams, and I have no idea how they will play out for the future, but I know there are some great things out there, and I can't wait to see what they are!

Tori, 19: My dreams for the future is to be a teacher and help transform students' lives in and out of the classroom.

Hannah, 18: I want to do something bigger than myself and make a difference in something. I plan to do that with teaching but I'm ready to go where ever I may be led.

MacKenzie, 21: My dreams for the future is truly becoming who I want to be and being happy in my life.

Discussion Questions for All Ages:

Do you take time to dream and imagine?

_____

_____

_____

_____

_____

How do you put your steps in place to achieve your dreams?

_____

_____

_____

_____

_____

Please share advice you would offer others about dreams and plans for the future:

_____

_____

_____

_____

_____

_____

_____

FOUR

Hurry, Hurry, Hurry

"Don't waste yourself in rejection, nor bark against the bad,
but chant the beauty of the good."
— Ralph Waldo Emerson (1803–1882)

I'm not sure how old I was when I realized that I had been in such a rush to get out of high school, complete college, and be out on my own…. I had wished so much time away. I remember a strong desire to begin a family of my own at a young age. For many of my friends, it was more the career that they were interested in. For some, the reward was to live on our own.

My family did not have the resources to send me away to college. This meant that I had to live at home and commute to the campus each day. I remember staying over for the orientation and wishing that I could have that experience for the next four years. The idea of getting to know a roommate and having parties in the dorm was thrilling. I was and continue to be a very social person.

In some ways, I made the most of living at home. I kept my job at a local department store. I spent most of my weekends and some of my weeknights with friends at favorite bars, and I dated quite a bit.

When I met my husband at a bar in the second semester of my freshman year, it never occurred to me that I would never have a place of my own. I still had this idea of being "That Girl." But after dating for a few years, my husband and I moved from our parents' homes into our first apartment right after our wedding.

As I read the answers that were submitted for this age group, I was surprised at some of them. Out of the answers to the first question in this category (Are you happily married or happily single right now?), eight young women were happily single with three in a committed relationship, six considered themselves happily married, and one unhappily single. I was thrilled to know that for these women, who ranged in age from twenty to twenty-eight, being single or married was working out well for them and there were very few who seemed lonely at this stage of life. For the next question regarding how friends might describe them, the responses were extremely positive.

I have included most of the answers from the second, third, and fourth questions because I found them to be powerful and inspiring. Many had already realized that they were people pleasers who needed to not worry so much about what others thought. I can honestly say that this did not occur to me much until I turned fifty.

Are you happily married or happily single right now?

Dayna, 26: I actually land right in between this question! I am joyfully engaged and ready to begin shared life with my fiancé in just a few months. The transition period is a mixture of striving for independence and understanding the hard, beautiful work of collaboration.

What words might a friend use to describe you?

Jessica, 24: Fun, outgoing, intelligent, logical, contagious

Lindsey: passionate, caring, put together

Bee: Creative, hard-working, good listener, sweet, helpful, smart, empathetic, high-achiever

Katie, 27: Friends would describe me as energetic, enthusiastic, loyal, kind, and intelligent.

Ashley, 24: I think a friend would describe me as loyal, compassionate, and honest.

Amanda, 20: Compassionate, caring, trustworthy, kind, dependable

Kayla, 22: Honest, resilient, determined, wild, empathetic, guarded

Melissa, 27: Outgoing, determined

Dayna, 26: Calm, grounded, joyful, present, loving

Hannah, 22: bubbly, energetic, boisterous, loud, enthusiastic, caring, kind

Hannah, 18: caring, loyal, compassionate, driven

Sarah: Dependable, strong, and self-motivated

Ashley, 20: outgoing, kind

Kelsey, 28: loyal, friendly, silly

What do you struggle with the most?

Jessica, 24: I would say my biggest struggle is knowing what I want and making choices that get me there. I have a tendency to want to make other people happy and for most of my life that meant making very few choices for me. In the past couple years I have really tried to focus on what makes me happy and where I want to be headed but it's something that doesn't come easily.

Lindsey: Feeling good about making choices that fit for who I am and not worrying about what other people think

Bee: Being an adult. What does that even mean? How do I pay off student loans and a car, apartment, utilities, and still feed myself? How do I find intelligent, eligible young men to date? What the hell am I doing with my life anyway? What are the big plans that God has for me, and what if they look different than the plans I have for me? Am I enough, really?

Katie, 27: Friends would describe me as energetic, enthusiastic, loyal, kind, and intelligent. I struggle the most with self-image. I have never had a positive self-image. Probably due to the people I have chosen to associate with my whole life that have made me feel like I was never good enough. I wake up every day and look in the mirror and groan, and then go on with my day.

Ashley, 24: I think the thing that I most struggle with is still feeling like I am in that transition age. I feel like I am still growing into an adult but people expect you to have your entire life figured out.

Amanda, 20: Trying to stay positive in midst of health

problems and trying not to worry about what tomorrow will bring.

Kayla, 22: Being satisfied with the now and not focusing/worrying about the future

Melissa, 27: Balancing personal and work life

Dayna, 26: I struggle with comparing my own journey to others. I want my life to be full of creativity, longing, and sustaining companionship, and I find myself quickly seeking the path others have successfully taken instead of deepening my own.

Hannah, 18: self-image, confidence

Ashtyn, 28: Perfectionism … and my health.

Hannah, 22: Confidence. I'm struggling to fit into a new career in a new city. I'm having a hard time finding my place both in the workplace and socially. I don't think I'm very good at my new job and I've really been struggling to find confidence at work. I've also been struggling to find good friends in this new town.

Sarah: Relying on others to get certain tasks done

Ashley, 20: Anxiety

Kelsey, 28: jealousy, gossip, worrying/anxiety

Discussion Questions for All Ages:

Do you feel as if you have rushed through some life experiences and then regretted that you didn't take time to savor the moments?

_____

_____

_____

_____

_____

_____

_____

How do you cherish the important times in your life now?

_____

_____

_____

_____

_____

What advice might you offer your younger self?

_____

_____

_____

_____

To feel rushed means...

_____

_____

_____

_____

_____

_____

What advice would you give your ten-year-old self?

Jessica, 24: Don't be a brat to your parents, one day you're going to realize how lucky you that they are yours.

Lindsey: Practice relaxing, and spending time on your own so it's not so hard when you're a grown up. Don't take yourself so seriously.

Bee: Enjoy childhood while you can; being an adult is hard. Middle school sucks, so just stay true to yourself and be nice to everyone.

Katie, 27: I would tell my ten-year-old self that it is okay to be smart and to only associate with people that build you up. I would also tell myself to enjoy every minute, because you never get being young and innocent back.

Ashley, 24: I would tell my ten-year-old self to be myself and do what I love. I feel like I wasted so much time on relationships that weren't positive or trying to do things for other people. I think I have finally learned that it's ok to do things that are for me and to make me happy.

Amanda, 20: People care more than they sometimes show

and not to worry about others opinions of me.

Anonymous: YOU CAN BE AN ARTIST IF YOU WANT TO BE (but mom is right, you won't make money)

Kayla, 22: Do what makes you happy. Don't do what you are supposed to do just because it is expected of you. Do what makes you happy regardless of other people's opinions or beliefs. You are the one who always has to live with your choices nobody else.

Anonymous: Listen to momma and trust your twenty something year old self when I say she truly does only want what's best for you.

Melissa, 27: Everyone is fighting some kind of battle. Don't be so quick to judge. You are the only one in charge of your happiness. Don't be afraid to give everything your all because that's the only way you will know how much you can truly achieve.

Dayna, 26: Your soon-to-be thick thighs are beautiful. You are worthy and beautiful. Stand strong in your own body and move yourself in good ways.

Hannah: life is awesome, take it slow and enjoy every minute of the ride.

Ashtyn, 28: Never forget how beautiful your heart is. You might not feel pretty, stylish, athletic, etc. but when you grow up, your family and friends won't care one bit about any of that. It's the love in your heart and the kindness that you show others that will matter the most. Besides, the opinions of others do not make you who you are. Also, don't forget to take care of yourself - physically, mentally, emotionally, and spiritually.

Hannah, 22: I guess it's kind of sad that I think the advice I needed to hear most when I was ten is the same advice I most need to hear today: Don't be afraid to be yourself. Be exactly you, no more, no less. Don't let others make you feel like you need to fit a mold. Don't compare yourself to others. You are not your sister and you are not your best friend so stop trying to become those people and let you be you. You are important. You really are special. There will be people that don't like you. That's ok, you don't need to impress them. Let them go. There are people who will always love you. (Hint: this is your family. Who, by the way, are not the lamest thing in the world, they're actually kind of awesome people.) You matter. The world would not be the same if you were not in it.

Sarah: Enjoy life, there is no rush to grow up. With everything being so strict with go to school, get good grades, go to college and earn a degree, then marriage and eventually a family. Life is meant to be enjoyed. As individuals it is OK to not fit in the cookie cutter of society, it is OK to be yourself.

Ashley, 20: STOP PLANNING. I always want things to go my way but sometimes I need to remind myself that gods plan is ALWAYS better than my own.

Kelsey, 28: Be you. It doesn't matter what you look like. Be kind and live your life and have fun.

Discussion Questions for All Ages:

How have the thoughts that others shared to this question helped you or made you think?

_____

_____

_____

_____

_____

What might you do differently now?

_____

_____

_____

_____

_____

Advice to my 10-year-old self:

_____

_____

_____

_____

_____

_____

_____

_____

_____

FIVE

A Love Beyond Measure

"The future belongs to those who believe in the beauty of their dreams."
—— Eleanor Roosevelt (1884–1962)

I wrapped up this chapter on my daughter Kelsey's twenty-eighth birthday. My son, Nick recently turned twenty-six, and I am not sure where this time has gone. I think that the most surprising thing about motherhood for me was the incredible instant love. I loved them when they were inside me, even in the many months of nausea and throwing up.... But nothing prepared me for that moment the baby is out, and the nurse put him or her in my arms or on my chest for the skin-to-skin contact. I remember looking into the eyes of my children and knowing that they knew me and how deeply I loved them already.

At that moment, you know that you would easily give your life for them. There is nothing more important than seeing them grow to be healthy, happy human beings. Now, don't get me wrong... I know I screwed up many times along the way, but almost always out of frustration or fear. There was no shortage of love in our household, even in the moments that we all were unlikeable.

I know that a woman of my age should say that her career was equally important, but for me, that would be a lie. Although I am sure there are times that my work seemed to take the front seat, I am also convinced that my kids knew that I would drop anything and everything if they needed me.

The questions that I asked of new moms come from the memories of this beautiful time in my life. I think it may have been the most disconnected time from my husband, in some aspects, but in some ways, it brought us to a much higher purpose together. The moments that they slept on him, or smiled so bright when seeing him after a long day can still melt my heart as I reminisce.

There will never be a time in my life that I feel I have done something this important. As I watch my daughter parent her two children now, I feel incredibly proud of the mother she has become.

NEW MOMS

What is the most surprising thing about being a mother?

Jessi: The love you find in the small things.

Franki, 37: I am actually surprised that I don't miss the freedom I had before I was a mom- when I could come and go whenever I wanted to. The best part of the day is when I get to come home to my little girl!

Brittany, 30: I am surprised on how much patience I have! It's totally different when it's your child crying.

Amanda, 29: I would say that the most surprising thing about being a new mom is how there isn't a second thought about putting someone else's need above your own.

Kelsey, 28: The overpowering love you immediately have for the children

Anonymous: Every day is something new and different!

Kelsey: How no matter what is happening, how much sleep you aren't getting, and every moment is absolutely amazing. You can't help but smile all the time.

Jocelyn: How much you can really love someone. I thought I knew love before but nothing compared to when I had my son. I never thought I would be a mom that would never want to leave her kids for anything, and now, I chose to spend the majority of my time with my family.

Discussion Questions for All Ages:

Please share your experience as a mom or a daughter:

_____

_____

_____

_____

_____

_____

_____

_____

_____

Have you found any relationships that are equally powerful?

_____

_____

_____

_____

_____

What advice might you offer a new mom?

_____

_____

_____

_____

_____

_____

_____

_____

_____

Thoughts about what a new mom is or an experienced mom is:

_____

_____

_____

_____

_____

What is the greatest challenge about being a mom?

Jessi: Feeling you might fail your children.

Franki, 37: Making time for myself. I still have a hard time doing things for myself- like exercising or going out with friends, book club, etc. my husband pushes me to get out without the baby and even though I fight him, he is right. I need to do things for me too.

Kelsey: All the pressure you get from everyone to do things certain ways. It makes it difficult to want to trust your motherly instincts.

Anonymous: Being responsible for molding this little being into a productive member of society.

Jocelyn: Not knowing if you're doing things the "right way" especially when dealing with discipline

Brittany, 30: I think it would be the waking up all night!

Amanda, 29: I would say the greatest challenge of being a mom is trying to balance all of life's responsibilities. As a working mother I want to do the best by my children, my clients, my coworkers, my husband and everyone else in my life and there isn't enough time in the day.

Kelsey, 28: Being a mom of two: Juggling my time with both of them to make sure they feel equally loved and important In general: wanting to be their best friend but knowing you need to be their "tough" parent as well.

What are the top three life lessons that you hope to teach your children?

Kelsey:

1. Believe in yourself
2. You can do anything you want in life

3. Family and God are most important

Jessi:

1. Be brave.
2. To be kind-hearted.
3. To have a relationship with The Lord.

Franki, 37:

1. I want her to know that she will never be alone. God will always be with her.
2. I want to teach her to be confident and to take risks in life. To not be afraid to try something new, even if it means failing.
3. I want to teach her to be open- minded and to not judge others.

Brittany, 30:

1. Believe in yourself.
2. Don't let anyone bring you down
3. The sky is the limit... always follow your dreams

Amanda, 29:

1. To love themselves no matter what
2. To show kindness and forgiveness to others in all situations.
3. To always try their best

Kelsey, 28:

1. Faith: Love of God. Knowing that there is a greater power watching over us
2. Family: Keeping them close they are the most important thing you have
3. Responsibility: Take responsibility for your actions and learn from them

Jocelyn:

1. Respect. To everyone but especially your elders. To me it's a valuable asset that isn't very often seen nowadays

2. Hard work. I want my children to know hard work pays off and that they shouldn't just wait for things to fall on their lap
3. Value of themselves. I want my children to understand that the only voice of judgment needs to be their own and they need to be kind to themselves. If you don't know your own value, they will be more susceptible to being hurt by others. They need to know what they bring to the table.

Anonymous:
1. Generosity, if you can see the needs in others and help with your time, talent or treasure that is a true blessing.
2. Delayed gratification, in a society where everything is instant I think it's going to be harder and harder for our children to learn true patients and delayed gratification.
3. Love God, love yourself and love others.

Discussion Questions for All Ages:

If you are a mom, what were your favorite mommy moments? Use the guide below to make an acrostic poem.

M _____

O _____

M _____

M _____

Y _____

M _____

O _____

M _____

E _____

N _____

T _____

S _____

SIX

The Tricky Years

"Beauty is in the eye of the beholder and it may be
necessary from time to time to give a stupid or
misinformed beholder a black eye."
— Miss Piggy

There are not many mothers of teenagers that I know
who don't feel an incredible shift at this time of life. For many
of us, the kids are not needing us nearly as much for the easy
things, but needing us more and more for the hard stuff. The
hard stuff might include discussions about sex, drugs and alcohol, friendships, testing the boundaries, and a myriad of other
emotional issues. I was fortunate to have a very open relationship with my own children, (in large part due to my work experience). We talked about relationships, spirituality, sexuality,
temptations, and more with relative ease.

I was blessed to have an inroad with them, as they had
seen many teenagers come to talk to me about these same issues over the years. I think that they knew that nothing would
shock me. For many parents (who don't have the training advantage that I did) this stage of life with growing children can

be changeling. At times, it is hard to trust and to give our kids the independence they are looking for. It is not only hard to trust their own judgments sometimes but also lend that trust to the people that they will be in contact with.

Whether you are a mom or not, there are additional challenges as well. We may get discouraged about what our bodies cannot do as easily these days. Many of us get frustrated about weight loss, hormone fluctuations, career decisions, and the body that seems to be unknown to us in many ways.

I remember having discussions with my sisters about who would pluck our chin hairs if we were ever in a coma. Topics that my seventeen-year-old self would never have imagined. This time of life offers a chance to reevaluate. As our kids become more independent, we begin to think about where we are in our own lives in terms of happiness and fulfillment. We might even offer advice that we wished we had taken in our younger years.

Friendships become so very important at this time of life. I know that when I am struggling through a day, time with a good friend can make all of the difference in the world. Cherish the time with those that might be experiencing some of the same confusion that you are.

30–45 YEAR OLDS

What are your strengths and weaknesses?

Jennifer: Strengths: seeming younger, art & design, easy to get to know weaknesses: struggle with fear, suck at body/health discipline, lazy/not a "do-er"

Anonymous: Strength—protecting my children.

Weakness—seeing my children hurt by friends and knowing I cannot protect them always.

Cathy: Strength—my faith, family and ability to assess a situation for what it is without emotional distraction. Weakness—wanting to complete too much too soon.

Anonymous: Strengths—creativity, openness to new adventures; weaknesses—I'm not consistent, I am emotional

Stef: Strengths: being a mom, being a good friend & wife, mediating conflict Weaknesses: guilt, anxiety, procrastination

Marta, 45: I think my strengths include being optimistic, joyful, content, loving and caring (Oh! And a hella bargain shopper). My weaknesses are being afraid of conflict, not being able to say what I mean, being fearful, and not taking action.

Anonymous: Strengths: good listener, humble, compassionate, passionate, open minded, great daughter, great friends. Weaknesses: too trusting, low self-esteem, not feeling good enough, poor choice in men.

Kristy, 38: I'm excited to see my boys grow up and for all that the future has in store for them. I'm excited to spend my future with my wonderful, amazing husband.

An G: Strengths: - dedicated - energetic - loyal - passionate - mentally strong - intuitive - good problem solver - influential - thorough - dependable Weaknesses: - jealous - stubborn - obsessive - revengeful - manipulative - easily shuns people - easily holds a grudge - insensitive to others - secretive - overbearing

Nadia: Strength—listening to others, writing, reading, being athletic, empathy, encouragement, ability to see the bright side of any situation while remaining real Weakness—perfectionist, spread myself too thin

Heather: strengths—kind, selfless. Weakness is I lose my sense of self identity because I am always putting people before myself. Lack of self-confidence.

Anna Grace, 36: Strengths: patience, ability to work with differently abled people, willingness to try.... Weaknesses: underestimating myself, meeting new people, fashion sense.

Discussion Questions for All Ages:

Do you admire strengths in others and yet not see your own?

_____

_____

_____

_____

_____

How do you let others know that you appreciate them and do you do the same for yourself?

_____

_____

_____

_____

_____

The best things about me are... The problem areas are...

_____

_____

_____

_____

What is something that you are excited for in the future?

Jennifer: I don't think about that very much. Summer time, vacation possibilities, having a fulfilling retirement one day, and "when I feel happy one day..."

Cathy: Stability. Seeing my children/nieces/nephews grow.

Anonymous: Moving back to the States

Stef: I'm excited to have another baby someday and raise my family with my wonderful husband.

Anonymous: Finding a job that I love

Marta, 45: I look forward to having grandchildren some-day, being an active part of my family. I look forward to a "new" relationship with my husband as my boys grow and move on. Hopefully we'll get to travel and make a new generation of memories for ourselves and our marriage.

Heather: Excited to watch my children grow and become happy individuals able to care for themselves.

Anonymous: Seeing my children grow up to be kind, productive adults

Becky, 37: The chance to travel and perhaps pursue further education of some sort.

Anna Grace, 36: The journey I am on... I feel like I've started this new journey about 3 years ago and look at the great things I've done in the past 3 years. I'm excited to see where the next many years take me!

Discussion Questions for All Ages:

What freedom do you have that you might not have anticipated?

_____

_____

_____

_____

_____

_____

How might you find ways to nurture your friendships more at this stage of life?

_____

_____

_____

_____

_____

_____

Freedom is... Nurturing is...

_____

_____

_____

_____

What is your favorite part about this middle stage of life?

Jennifer: I have gotten to a point in my career where I'm happy doing what I do. My kiddos aren't babies anymore, so they are more manageable.

Anonymous: Seeing the joy in my children's eyes as they discover new things. Also as they learn new information.

Anonymous: Being a parent and having the means to travel.

Stef: Having kids is the most amazing thing and my husband and I are so lucky to have this opportunity.

Marta, 45: Feeling confident in who I am, what I stand for. Watching my children grow and become independent, strong and amazing individuals.

Anonymous: Giving birth to my daughter.

Kristy, 38: I'm beyond all the drama of my teenage and young adult years, and I am able to enjoy life for what it is. I finally feel like I can be who I really feel I am without fear of what others have to say.

An G: Not caring what other people think about me.

Heidi: A bit wiser. More free time. Comfortable with myself.

Nadia: The fact that I am can do and say what I want and understand the consequences. I am more aware of who I am and the person God wants me to be.

Heather: The ability to make decisions and help guide my family.

Anonymous: Spending time with my "surprise" toddler. 10.5 years after my first son.

Becky, 37: Watching my kids grow and slowly become their own little independent people! And getting to spend a bit more time with my husband as the kids become busier with their own lives.

Anna Grace, 36: Being able to pay attention to my "wants" as well as my "needs!" Spent so many years trying to get by and now am finally at a place that I can enjoy life!

What is your greatest fear?

Jennifer: That I won't ever feel like I'm making the most of the life I've been given.

Anonymous: Mid age crisis for me and/or my spouse

Cathy: The loss of my kids.

Anonymous: Dying while my child is young

Stef: Letting others down, not being able to provide a deserving childhood for my son

Marta, 45: Complacency. Also, losing my family and faith, losing good health.

Anonymous: Loneliness

Kristy, 38: That something will happen to my children or my husband.

Heidi: My kids hating me for my past mistakes.

Nadia: Losing my memories

Heather: My greatest fear is death. This is something I need to become at peace with. I fear losing the ones I love through death or growing apart.

Becky, 37: Losing people that I love.

Anna Grace, 36: Disappointing someone I love, misunderstandings, being Lonely.

Discussion Questions for All Ages:

How do you handle your fears and what have you learned about fear?

_____

_____

_____

_____

_____

Write a poem about "It's never too late…"

_____

_____

_____

_____

_____

_____

_____

_____

_____

_____

_____

_____

_____

_____

SEVEN

Finding Our Way (Again!)

"Beauty is in the eye of the beholder and it may be
necessary from time to time to give a stupid or
misinformed beholder a black eye."
— Miss Piggy

Lately, I have thought more and more about what mark I would like to leave on the world, on my children, and grandchildren. I know that I want to own the mistakes that I have made and let them help me to be better, kinder, and more compassionate. Retirement still seems a long way away, but for many friends of mine, it is happening in their late fifties and early sixties. There are days that I find myself looking in the mirror and wondering when "that" happened. Laugh lines, more than frown lines are appearing on my face and I am trying not to get too hung up on them.

More than what I see in the mirror, it is hard for me to imagine not having a place to work on a regular basis. What will that mean if I am no longer needed? How do I make my mark on the world if I am not gainfully employed? Will my spouse make me crazy if we have too much time together? Will

I want to be with my grandchildren as much as I think I will? How will this affect me financially?

As I ponder all of the questions, I cannot help but to get excited about the extra time to follow my dreams. I think about all of the ways that I could volunteer my time, how clean my house might be, that I might finally get some of my books published.... I was especially appreciative of the answers that women were willing to share in this chapter.

AGE 46 TO RETIREMENT

What is the biggest change in your life?

Katie: Divorce

Gwen: Body

Brenda, 55: Focusing on work.

Anonymous: Being responsible for aging parents who have dementia.

Jenny, 46: My husband suffering from kidney failure at age 46.

Sonja: I'm sitting on the brink of having my first child go off to college. I'm excited for him but struggling to let him go. In my eyes he is still my baby. I have been responsible for him for almost 18 years. How do you wake up one day and just say, "He's on his own and no longer my responsibility?" It leaves a hole in my heart... while simultaneously being oh so proud of him.

Frances: Falling in love again at the age of 49. The difference in the love that you have at this age as opposed to when you are a teenager. Lots of the same butterflies and excitement, but a more mature relationship. I love the emphasis on the talking and the laughter!

June: Becoming an empty nester.

Tami: The biggest change is the transition in realizing my kids are growing up so fast, parenting goals have redirected to more life lessons and guidance for them to learn, out into play so when the time comes to be on their own, they are as ready as they can be. It seems once they get middle/high school they need just as much attention as when they were little, but in a different way.

Cathy, 56: Quitting my job, selling my house and taking a year off to travel.

Pam: The biggest change is no longer having children at home.

Karen: going from a full house to an almost empty nest

Beverly: anticipating empty nest. What should I do? I want to make the rest of my life have eternal value, using the unique gifts that God has given me, gifts that have stayed on the back burner for so long. Hopefully they are not burned up.

Anonymous: Making the decision in my early 20s to end a surprise pregnancy (long before Roe v. Wade).

Tracey, 53: Giving birth to my son.

Cathy: I am a breast cancer survivor. I was diagnosed with aggressive cancer at age 45 and am celebrating my 10-year anniversary in August 2015. Having cancer opened doors and provided opportunities I would have never experienced otherwise. I met some incredible women and men during my journey, have served on the annual Surviving and Thriving Breast Cancer Awareness Luncheon committee and volunteered with the American Cancer Society's Reach to Recovery program. It's my pleasure to emotionally support others going through a difficult time.

Virginia, 50: the biggest change in my life has to do with family. Kids going off into the world and now helping take care of a parent.

Alex: Becoming a mother and having to be responsible for the nurturing of another human.

Linda: Being an "empty nester." It seems that I always focused on my children, and now that they are living their own lives, I really don't seem to have much of a purpose anymore. I keep really busy doing things I love to do, but still feel like I am floundering at times.

Sylvia: Leaving my spouse and the military lifestyle that I loved

Patty, 54: Husband passing away, and being alone.

Laurie, 56: My biggest change so far was from age 32 to 35 years when I got divorced, met my current husband, had another child & got remarried.

Anonymous: the biggest change was my husband dying at age 40 & my world was turned upside down, nothing was as I expected & I had to start all over in a new life that I was not at all prepared for.

Elspeth, 51: Getting divorced after 30 years of marriage, starting a new relationship with a Junior High School friend, and changing my career from floor nursing to management.

Sharon, 54: The biggest change in my life up to this point was when all of our kids moved out of the house and it was just myself and my husband. For the past 30 years it had been us and the kids, everything revolved around them; their wants and needs. All of a sudden the kids were gone, the whirlwind of life with kids had stopped, and it was just the two of us. With the kids gone there was this big void in my life; no more school events to attend, doctor appointments to schedule, youth group meetings to get to, etc. It has been a tough adjustment, I am still trying to figure it out. Also with the kids gone, it has made me realize how much my husband and I have neglected our marriage. The kids were our main focus so it was easy to put "us" on hold, now we have to work on being a couple again.

Ellen, 50: Accepting the fact that I will probably never get married.

Sharon: Having so much free time to do what I want to do. Having four children meant most of my time was spent caring for them or attending their activities. Now I have much more time to pursue other interests.

Discussion Questions for All Ages:

How have you adjusted your schedule or life in a way that meets your needs?

_____

_____

_____

_____

_____

How do you plan to spend extra time you will have?

_____

_____

_____

_____

_____

What is your greatest worry about changes at this stage of life?

_____

_____

_____

_____

_____

Write about packing away some memories and creating new ones:

_____

_____

_____

_____

_____

Do you remember what you hoped to be when you were ten or twelve years old? Did that change over the years?

Deborah: I wanted to be a doctor. My dad died my senior year in College and made medical school impossible, which was fine because 4 years later, I married a great man.

Katie: I wanted to be a teacher and a mom. I didn't travel the path I thought I would, but I have actually achieved both.

Brenda, 55: I did not realize my dream of being a flight attendant. I have been VERY fortunate to travel a whole bunch in the last 6 years of my life. The dream is still there but fading fast.

Jenny, 46: I remember wanting to be happily married with a couple of kids, and have been blessed in both requests.

Sonja: I always wanted to be an architect. I ended up getting my degree in interior design which is very similar. I worked in that field for 12 years but was not fulfilled. I returned to school and became a nurse. It's never too late to change your mind.

Anonymous: Musician. Yes.

June: I wanted to be a veterinarian. I spent 20 some years in the human medical field and finally, starting at the age of 46, I started working at a veterinarian clinic. (Happy Face)

Tami: I always thought I would just be a housewife at that age, was fascinated with medicine but did not know what I wanted to do back then. Now, I am a working housewife with a medical career. I guess I got the best of both worlds, although it is challenging at times to find the balance.

Cathy, 56: Wife and mother. Never married with no children.

Pam: I wanted to be a teacher which I'm not and very thankful for that. What I do is even better! I do work in the public schools as an Occupational Therapist treating students with special needs.

Karen: Physical therapist aid. I work with children instead.

Beverly: I didn't really have any dreams, except to some-day be a grandmother. I was a little concerned that in order to be a grandmother I had to be a mother, and to be a mother I had to be a wife, and to be a wife I had to at least LIKE boys. That was a major obstacle! Now I am a wife and mother with 4 kids, 3 of whom are adults. I've done my part. Now I wait. My most persistent dish bubbling on the back burner is for me to be involved in storytelling through creative arts. Not sure what that should look like for me, or if I could make any money with it as a career.

Tracey, 53: I only wanted to be married, with children. Sadly, I am not married; however, I do have a beautiful son.

Cathy: I wanted to be a teacher, I think. As career choice time grew near I realized that was not my calling and have loved the path I actually chose.

Alex: I wanted to be an oceanographer. I didn't get much encouragement from my parents to attend college and by the time I was college-age I was too afraid to leave home to get an education.

Linda: I always wanted to be a mom, and that has turned out well for me.

Sylvia: I don't remember thinking about this. I think I was just busy being a kid.

Ann, 52: I don't remember, but did decide to go into Nursing in high school, and have stayed an RN for 30 years. Wasn't really planning on getting married and having a child, but did it anyways. I never had looked at bridal magazines or planned my dream wedding. It was also 10 years into our marriage that we had a kid.

Laurie, 56: I wanted to be an Elementary school teacher & I did get my degree in education, was certified to teach & there were no jobs due to massive layoffs in the state where I lived. I have taught in preschool, directed daycares, was a Corporate Trainer & now train for a state organization, but have never taught in Elementary schools.

Jesse: Yes. I did change career directions in college from law to non-profit. But, I am not sorry that I did.

Elspeth, 51: I wanted to be a marine biologist and work at SeaWorld. I am a nurse of 32 years so I will have to say the marine biologist did not work out. But I am grateful that it didn't work out. Nursing was my calling from God and I answered. I have helped a few souls come into the world and helped many leave this world. Being in healthcare and studying the body has opened my eyes to fact that we are not just an accident but rather a beautifully created human.

Gwen: I wanted to be able to take in all the stray animals and care for them. We have one cat he was a stray.

Sharon, 54: Unfortunately I do not remember what I wanted to be later in life, at the age of 10 or 12.

Virginia, 50: I think I wanted to be a veterinarian when I was that age. I'm a music therapist and teacher now. Love my 3 cats and dog, though!

Ellen, 50: I think I wanted to be a writer and/or a detective. I manage a team of financial investigators who write reports for the government so I'm at least in the ballpark.

Sharon: I wanted to be a teacher from the age of six and that is what I became and what I am still doing. I love being a teacher!

Frances: I wanted to be a backup singer in a band! I have found lots of ways to include music in my life but I am always in awe of the people that can move you to goosebumps with a beautiful voice and presence.

Discussion Questions for All Ages:

How did your career mold you into the woman you are now?

_____

_____

_____

_____

_____

Do you have any regrets about what you might have done differently?

_____

_____

_____

_____

_____

Make a list of pre-career ambitions and post-career ambitions

Pre:_____

_____

_____

_____

_____

_____

Post:_____

_____

_____

_____

_____

_____

What were some of the best life lessons you learned along the way?

_____

_____

_____

_____

_____

What is the most surprising part of this time of life?

Brenda, 55: The biggest surprise for me at this point in my life is that I feel fulfilled without being a full time mom anymore and without being overly active in a church environment. I am surprised that I don't miss all the things that have seemed so important to me for a huge portion of my life. I am finding great satisfaction in my work productivity and making time for friends old and new when I can.

Deborah: How much I miss my sons. We have them for a short period of time, then they grow up and move on. They are interesting young men and I miss our discussion and time together.

Katie: Looking ahead I always thought that life would feel pretty settled and easy at this stage of my life — that I would have it all figured out. Not even close! Although I do have a much better sense of self than I imagined.

Jenny, 46: The most surprising part of this time in life is that I am still insecure about myself sometimes.

Sonja: I had no idea how hard it would be to be a mother to a teenager. You always hear about the difficulties of late night infant feelings or 2-year-old temper tantrums. But no one truly prepares you for the time when your teenagers push away from you and make risky decisions and yet you are still responsible for them... and love them to the depths of your soul.

Anonymous: The fact that I have trouble figuring how to mangle my career right now.

June: That I decided to get my body more physically fit.

Tami: The emotional part of it! Reality hits hard at this age!!!

Cathy, 56: I am having trouble accepting that I can't do some of the things I used to be able to do. I thought I would accept these changes more gracefully.

Pam: The most surprising thing about this time in my life is that I am single. I was divorced over 10 years ago and haven't found a significant other yet.

Karen: How fast time goes by

Beverly: Realizing that I have reached the age of those I considered role models 20 years ago. It is good to discover that I actually have gleaned some wisdom over the years.

Anonymous: Finding new love at age 71.

Tracey, 53: The feeling of freedom.

Cathy: Transitioning from working a 50 hour a week responsible-for-outcomes job as the Director of Marketing for a DME company to realizing my dream of living on the lake.

Years of hard work have paid off We used to vacation in rental lake houses. Now I feel like I'm on vacation every day!

Alex: I still feel young in body and spirit and that the best is yet to be.

Linda: Having the freedom to do things that I have always wanted to do!

Sylvia: The news that I am going to be a grandmother, unexpected but wonderful nevertheless.

Ann, 52: Trying to balance everything, and realizing that I have gotten older. I still have my parents to care for, and a teenager to raise. I am lucky to work part time, but hate to do the stuff grownups do — clean the house, cook meals, weed the garden, etc. And, while I am not sure what age I am in my mind, I am no longer young.

Laurie, 56: That even though my husband & I are empty nesters, we are still incredibly busy. I don't know how we ever got things done & raised kids.

Elspeth, 51: That you can fall madly, deeply in love again.

Gwen: How quickly it came and how much I miss children who are not in this area now.

Sharon, 54: I am surprised by how much I miss being a mom. I used to think I could hardly wait until the kids were out on their own, doing their own thing and I would have time to do what I wanted to. Now that time has come and I really do miss doing the mom stuff. This is all fairly new for me, and in time I will adjust and figure out what it is I want to do in the next half of my life, but I really didn't expect this phase to be this difficult.

Patty, 54: How relaxed I am with myself and not worried about what people think about me.

Virginia, 50: that I don't really care if someone has a problem with me. I do my best in life and am okay with that. I'm also surprised that time continues to accelerate.

Ellen, 50: How crappy I feel most of the time. I took health for granted when I was younger, but now between the diabetes and the arthritis and the weight gain and menopause things are so much more difficult than I thought they would be physically-speaking.

Frances: Being in love like a schoolgirl but also appreciating our differences and how much I want to give now.

Sharon: That I don't really miss the life I had when I was younger. I loved every minute of raising my family, but I am enjoying this part of my life too.

Discussion Questions for All Ages:

What do you like the best about yourself right now?

_____

_____

_____

_____

_____

Is there anything that you feel like you missed doing with your children when they were younger?

_____

_____

_____

_____

I wish I had... Right now I'm great at...

_____

_____

_____

_____

_____

"Look Grandma, it's a Princess"

"Far away in the sunshine are my highest aspirations. I may not reach them, but I can look up and see their beauty, believe in them, and try to follow where they lead." —Louisa May Alcott (1832–1888)

I will never forget the day in Florida that I was with my granddaughter Lauryn, two years old at the time, and we were playing in the pool at the condo where we spent our April vacations. She was friendly with everyone, and absolutely loved all people from the time she was a baby. A woman walked in with a long sundress - if I had to guess I would say she was well into her seventies. Lauryn who was in a crazy Disney phase at the time, said, "Look, Grandma, it's a Princess!" I watched that woman light up like a Christmas tree. Then I thought to myself, "It doesn't matter how old we are, most of us still want to be treated like and look like the princess of our dreams and childhood fantasies." I am guessing that the woman she complimented felt like a princess for the rest of that day, week, or maybe even longer.

As I have reached an age where my body is changing in

so many ways (more weight gain, adult acne, facial hair, raging mood swings), I cannot help but to wish I had known some things earlier that might have helped me along the way.

Some of the lessons that I wish I had learned in my younger years are:

- Never stop playing outside
- Keep moving and fighting the urge to nap
- Eat when you're hungry and don't make it your escape from _____ (Well, for me, that is EVERYTHING)
- When you are joyful, you are beautiful
- Women need to build each other up rather than tear each other down

I am sure there are one hundred more lessons, but I know that you can come up with many as well. The questions for retired women are designed to help us understand one another better, no matter our age or stage in life. There is much to be learned from their insight.

RETIRED WOMEN

If you could change one thing about your life, what would that be?

Carol, 76: That I didn't take better care of myself, while I was caring for others.

Michael: don't be afraid of new things

Josie: my relation with sons

Sherrie, 66: I don't think I would change anything about my life because everything I did, good or bad, helped to make me the woman I am. Just as an example, I always wished I had been able to attend college but due to my father's disabling accident my family couldn't afford it. If I had gone to college I probably wouldn't have met my wonderful husband and I wouldn't change that for anything. God has a plan and we learn and grow from all our experiences. The tears as well as the laughter are all a part of our lives.

Anonymous: my work with my church

Charlotte, 60: Be satisfied with myself at a younger age!

Discussion Questions for All Ages:

Have you ever made a life altering choice that you wish you could do over?

_____

_____

_____

_____

_____

_____

Is there anything that you wish you had known about at a younger age?

_____

_____

_____

_____

_____

Gosh, I wish someone had told me... Some of the crazy decisions I make over the years are...

_____

_____

_____

_____

_____

What is the most joyful part of your life right now?

Carol, 76: Family

Michael: loving my children, grandchildren and great grandchildren

Josie: church

Anonymous: calming down; taking things as they come

Charlotte, 60: My Family, mostly my Grandchildren!

Sherrie, 66: The most joyful part of my life now is the blessing of time with my family. I am retired and have been able to help out my parents as well as my father-in-law. I get to spend time with my children and grandchildren on a regular basis and being retired allows me time to travel to see the ones who are out of town. I also have a large extended family who are a joy to spend time with. Many people don't have the great bond with their family that I do and it is truly a blessing for me.

Discussion Questions for All Ages:

At what age did you feel most joyful, and why?

_____

_____

_____

_____

What do you do on a regular basis that makes you happy?

_____

_____

_____

_____

I am most happy when...

_____

_____

_____

_____

Happiness in retirement is...

_____

_____

_____

_____

What age did you really enjoy and why did you love it so much?

Carol, 76: I loved the early twenties when I was a young mother.

Michael: my 40's because my children were at an age that they did not need constant care and I could listen to my inner self more

Charlotte, 60: My 50's, I actually felt good about myself and the direction I was going!

Sherrie, 66: I have lived through so many different ages it is hard to choose. I really loved being a stay-at-home mom with my 2 daughters but I think it was most fun being a grandmother of 3 wonderful kids. It was fun experiencing each age of their childhood without having all the responsibilities of parenthood. You know the old saying "spoil them and send them home." I get to share so many of my favorite experiences with them as well as sharing in all their activities.

What did you like the most about yourself and your life at that age?

Carol, 76: I believe that I felt most fulfilled caring for my little ones.

Michael: I was trying to be the person I knew my mother would have liked.

Josie: starting out on my own

Charlotte, 60: I felt comfortable in my own skin, I felt like I finally realized what was the most important things were in my life, my family and friends. Money and things don't matter!

Sherrie, 66: I really liked being a young Grandmother. I was a mother at 20 and always felt like I grew up with my children. I became a grandmother at 44 and felt that I had the experience and knowledge necessary to be a good one but also was young enough to enjoy playing and being active with my grandchildren. I certainly couldn't picture my grandmothers doing many of the things that I did with my grandchildren. I think I was probably more relaxed with them as well because I didn't have all the stress parents are going through. I also had accepted who I am as a person. My personality as well as my physical appearance. You can always make changes but you have to accept the things you can't change.

Discussion Questions for All Ages:

What do you like the best about the age you are right now?

_____

_____

_____

_____

_____

What age do you think women feel the most secure?

_____

_____

_____

_____

Women begin to feel secure when...

_____

_____

_____

_____

QUESTIONS FOR ALL AGES

What do you value the most about who you are right now and your place in the world?

Maddie, 13: I value life itself because I know that without it, I wouldn't even be here. But more than anything, I value the ability to be unique and make my own mark on the world. If we were all the same, it would be an unbelievably boring place to live but with everyone being their own person, things become more interesting with shared and differing interests defining our relationships and our lives.

Anonymous: That I have a big heart, and my family and friends are very important to me

Jocelyn: I value my helping hand. I believe that we should help whoever needs our help. I would like to believe that I've made a footprint in this world by helping and passing that lesson along to who I've helped.

Anonymous: I am in the place God put me and (trying to) being a shining light for him

Frances: I think it is an awareness of how important it is to use the gifts that God blessed me with and to have someone in my life that sees that most beautiful part of me.

Dayna, 26: I value that I'm deepening my skills to show up with and for people through graduate studies in social work. I am on the edge of transition with school and marriage, and yet I am deeply satisfied by the ways I have sustained myself to be whole and loving.

Anonymous: I am a mom of young girls. That's never going to happen again. I enjoy all the ups and downs that comes with being a working mom of girls.

Emily, 19: I value the fact that I feel like I'm a good, beautiful person who has a lot to live for and a lot to look forward to.

Anonymous: I value all of my talents, hobbies, and free time.

Anonymous: My immediate family needs me / loves me; I have everything I need; I try to do good things for others, and I'm starting to recognize what I need to do in my own life to get where I want to be.

Abby, 18: Right now I value the fact that I am able to discover and decide who I am for myself, without any ties. I love being able to be in college, meeting people, and doing new things.

Jessi: The thing I value most, about how I am right now, is that I am grateful. The life lessons that come with being a parent, they taught me to truly be grateful for every day.

Anonymous: I appreciate and value the perspective that I have on life. I'm able to be joyful for other people's success.

Amanda, 20: I feel confident about who I am and my college plans. And I'm trying to trust that what I want my life to look like and how it will actually happen will be different, but it will all be okay.

Katie, 27: The thing I value most about who I am at this point in life is the start of my role as a new wife and a dog mommy. I also love all of the work I do with kids in the school, but my family is most important.

Becky, 37: I value my role as wife and mother the most. And I value knowing that there is a God who brings people together for certain times and places for the glory of His kingdom.

Kristy, 38: That I am able to be supportive of others.

Jessica, 24: Being authentic. I have never been the kind of person who felt like they were pretending to be something or someone they weren't. I was almost always comfortable in my own skin and I genuinely liked who I was (for the most part) and in the last few years I have realized how unusual that is for people and especially girls. Realizing this made it very clear to me that I wanted to love people of all shapes and sizes, I want all girls to have the positive feelings I had growing up and I think a lot of that came from being true to myself and having people around me who supported me to be as loud and strange as I felt. At the age I am now I do my best to encourage the people around me to be who they are no matter what and I do everything in my power to do the same.

Alex, 53: I'm happy, truly happy and for the first time it isn't a fleeting feeling. I'm loving and kind and that is my purpose.

Sylvia: I value being at peace with who I have become, the thought that career-wise this is where I want to be and I am not hankering to climb the career ladder any higher. I am valuing time over career and looking forward to retirement.

Ann, 52: I feel like I am doing alright, and am a good person. I try to be helpful however possible, with my time, my talents and my money. I have a wonderful family, and am loved.

Kayla, 22: I value the job that I have and my career goals. I also value my love of doing new things even if they scare me.

Anna Grace, 36: I value having the love and trust of people that I look up to. I value my impact on the world, whether it be a small impact for a brief second or a larger impact that lasts over time.

Anonymous: I can stand on my own merits and rarely let other people's opinion of me or my choices matter. They can take me as I am, warts and all. They can like me or not. I can take or leave what I do for a living. Wisdom definitely comes with age.

Hannah, 18: I value my drive to do the best I can. I feel like I have to be the best I can in order to keep up with everything in the world. It's all so different and I feel like I need to do everything I can to keep up.

Anonymous: Right now I value most that I embrace different ideas and keep an open mind. Right now I value most my place in my family and in my team at school, since those are the two places where I feel accepted.

Amanda, 29: My kindness towards others and the way in which I am able to interact with all sorts of people difference then myself.

MacKenzie, 21: I value most about myself is that I am always willing to help everybody and sharing my compassion.

Caitlin, 14: I value most that I am the future of our world. This generation is going to rule the world one day and I am glad to be a part of it!

Discussion Questions for All Ages:

To value is to...

_____

_____

_____

_____

_____

_____

_____

What has been your greatest challenge regarding your appearance and your personality?

MacKenzie, 21: The challenge that I face with my appearance is my weight and getting healthy. As for my personality the greatest challenge not being judgmental and negative.

Jocelyn: My greatest challenge regarding my appearance is my weight. I've always struggled with it and I think it's the biggest insecurity I have. I'm outgoing and friendly but when I feel uncomfortable with how I look I become very timid and quiet.

Maddie, 13: The greatest challenge I've faced regarding my appearance is my weight because I know that I'm not as skinny as I'd like to be and as skinny as my friends but I've realized that size doesn't matter if I'm Healthy. The biggest challenge with my personality was knowing that some people might find it weird or view it as "wrong" but I also realized that there is no "wrong" because it's who I am and not something that I can change.

Anonymous: I think that in my Catholic school with uniforms I can't express my own clothing style.

Brenda, 55: I have really not been that concerned with appearance in my life. I am who I am and others can take me or leave me. Perhaps my attitude toward appearance was shaped by the fact that I was bullied in 6th and 7th grade for that very reason. I was a late bloomer and others found it entertaining, perhaps, to pick on me for that. I had to learn for "survival" that it really didn't matter what others thought. I developed a thick skin pretty quickly. It took until I was 35, though, to understand that the most important relationship in my life is with Jesus, my Savior. I know he is happy with me and, even though there is always room for improvement, He loves me exactly as I am. I learned that if there are things about myself I want to change, today is the day. Tomorrow may never come.

Abby, 18: I have always been quiet, so it has been a lot of work to sort of overcome that. It took a long time for me to be comfortable talking to people I didn't know very well, but after my concussion, I realized that I was missing out on my life because of my fear, so I decided to change myself.

Amanda, 20: I've always been told I'm beautiful and most days I believe it but some days are hard and it's hard to think about feeling beautiful. As for my personality, I don't always feel worthy of talking about myself and my feelings. Even when I know I need to talk to someone, I sometimes feel like I'm wasting their time.

Emily, 19: I have had trouble feeling comfortable with my weight. I'm relatively small in stature, so when I gain weight it is very obvious to me. I lifeguard and I get nervous come summer about wearing a swimsuit if I haven't been exercising as much as I should or if I've gained a little bit of weight recently.

Katie, 27: My greatest challenge is my weight. I think that at this point I don't even care about clothes or hair or make up. I know that even if I put in a ton of effort, I still won't like how I look on the other side, so why bother?

Becky, 37: Appearance- realizing that "healthy" and "weight" are not equivalent. At 5'9", I will never be a size 4 or weigh 120 pounds. And realizing that who I am as a person is not tied to my weight or appearance. Personality—I'm fairly social, but am introverted enough that I am sometimes awkward in conversations with large groups or people I don't know. I either don't talk at all, or I talk too much depending on my mood... I've learned to accept that this is just who I am, and it doesn't bother me as much anymore.

Kristy, 38: My greatest challenge with my personality has been my introversion. My greatest challenge with my appearance has been my physical fitness and my weight.

Jessica, 24: From a very young age I struggled with my height and weight. I was never small, the word petite has never been a word that applied to me. And in many ways my height has always been an advantage; people listen when you speak, you stand out in a crowd, you rarely have to ask for help getting things, but as a kid standing out was never the goal, fitting in was. I always wanted to be the small girl, the girl who fit in every piece of clothing, the girl who everyone called "cute." It took about 22 years for me to realize that no one loves every part of themselves but that doesn't mean you have to hate parts, sometimes you just have to remind yourself of the value that the differences have. Being tall may have stunted my dating game for a while, but it evened the playing field and gave me a confidence it took me a long time to understand.

Alex, 53: Sadly, I have spent too much time worrying about my weight, but I just want to be the healthiest I can be now. I used to worry about if people liked me, but the older I get the less I care. I don't want to change who I am to fit someone else's ideal.

Frances: To remember that I am most beautiful when I am doing something I am passionate about. I wish I could have more confidence when my partner notices the things that make me shine and sees so much beauty that I don't see.

Sylvia: My weight as far as appearance. Sometimes I feel like a dinosaur when it comes to work ethic, I easily get aggravated with people who do not share the same work ethic as me. I believe this is a sign that retirement should come sooner rather than later.

Ann, 52: Appearance wise, it's been my weight and my lack of exercise, which has led me to be very out of shape and inflexible. I hate having to get down on my hands and knees—getting up is hard! Personality wise, I feel comfortable with who I am, and my beliefs. I try to speak my mind, instead of holding my tongue. It doesn't bother me to not be "part of the crowd"... I never was and never will be. But I used to be quieter, and not let others know that I felt and thought differently. I am also comfortable enough with myself to be alone—I don't need someone else to define me.

Anna Grace, 36: Appearance always is affected by my depression. When I'm depressed, I don't care how I look. But I've also found that when I'm depressed it helps a lot to take care of my appearance. Looking good helps me feel better and seems to help me find my way out of depression. Personality—I struggle with a recent diagnosis of ADHD. To me it comes with a stigma. It causes me to do things that I don't feel like I have control over (interrupt people, unintentionally "one up", etc.). Sometimes comes across as rude and I don't like to consider myself a rude person. I work on this every day!

Dayna, 26: My greatest challenge has been accepting the parts of myself that aren't as small—my thighs, my nose, my diminishing abs. However, when I shifted my thought process to understand that these attributes make me fuller, I felt freed.

Hannah, 18: With my appearance I always feel so ostracized with my height. Everyone says that it's so nice and how they wish they were taller but have always felt awkward being the tall girl. I feel that has played into my personality too because I feel like since I'm tall I need to have a smaller personality to be normal. I guess I just want to fit in and be friends with everyone and I cannot.

Amanda, 29: My appearance would be that I never no matter what feel like I am pretty enough, whether it is my weight, my makeup, my hair or my skin I just never feel enough. Personality I would say I don't feel challenged in that way.

Caitlin, 14: My greatest challenge honestly is not being over-emotional. I have quite the short temper (it's genetic) and I have a hard time not showing it.

Discussion Questions for All Ages:

My footprints through time are...

_____
_____
_____
_____

My Hallmark card to the world would be:

_____
_____
_____
_____

Fighting vanity is...

_____
_____
_____
_____

What does dressing for success look like?

_____
_____
_____
_____

What impact have your faith/ spiritual beliefs had on your life?

Anonymous: I've wanted to be a better person for the church kids I work with. And being a volunteer has kept me going to church. And that keeps my family going to church a little too. And teaching Sunday school has helped me see that all Christians believe that we should "do good things for others". And that's what life is about.

Brenda, 55: God has carried me through some extremely rough valleys. Knowing that His plan is always to prosper me and not to harm me, keeps me going. Having faith in His plans and not my own are paramount. When I am willing to surrender that to Him, great things happen.

Anonymous: Carried me through hard times and kept me level-headed during the good times.

Abby, 18: My faith, and the people who have helped my faith to grow, have been instrumental in making me who I am today. Deciding what I believe took a while, and learning to see God in the little things has been a process, but now, I know that I will always have my faith to fall back on, even if everything else goes wrong. My faith and God are things that I know will always be there and even if I drift away, I'll always be welcomed home again. Right now I value the fact that I am able to discover and decide who I am for myself, without any ties. I love being able to be in college, meeting people, and doing new things.

MacKenzie, 21: My faith has always been something that has come easy and has always been near. I think having an amazing faith has made me a better person all around.

Anonymous: God is my strong tower. I run to him and

find shelter, my very present help in time of need...and...There but for the grace of God go I. Let justice and grace become my embrace.

Amanda, 20: My faith has been the groundwork for my life. It's helped me stay positive when I've been depressed. And it's rewarding to know I can talk to God when I don't know who else to talk to.

Emily, 19: My faith is the foundation of my life. All of my problems and concerns go to God and I feel like I have a really great relationship with God. He influences everything I do and helps me through anything I struggle with.

Anonymous: I am a Unitarian Universalist. I believe in bringing an open heart to anyone I meet.

Becky, 37: My faith reminds me daily that I was created to be just who I am, and that God loves me exactly as I am. It also reminds me that we are put on this earth to love God and love others. It's a bit of a tough thing to remember in this narcissistic age of selfies and instant gratification, but my faith has taught me that God delights in His people loving other people.

Kristy, 38: My faith has helped me accept me for who I am just as God accepts me with all my faults. It has also brought me into the presence of people who will lift me up when needed, and give me the support to keep going.

Anonymous: My faith reminds me that I'm loved beyond belief regardless of how I feel about myself on any given day.

Frances: I love to look at the world and see God at work in so many ways. When a friend is feeling lost or alone I pray and almost always there is a sign or a God moment that gives me the right way to encourage.

Jessica, 24: Faith is always something I felt like I struggled with more than the rest of my family. My sisters always just seemed to know what it was they thought and felt, while my head was filled with far more doubts. Being close to them at a young age tended to make it even harder because I felt like I was doing something wrong, being close to them again now and being able to have deep, meaningful conversations I've come to find that my doubt and confusion has much more to do with "religion" as an organization than my faith. At my core I know that having faith and believing in something more is what drives me. Growing up with people who pushed me to care about others, to accept, to love, made me who I am.

Alex, 53: Faith has been an interesting and challenging part of my life. It has lifted me up high and sometimes it has sent me to the depths of sadness. I'll always have questions that there are no clear answers to.

Anonymous: I believe fully in faith and God has blessed me more times than I can count.

Katie, 27: My faith keeps me going. It helps bring me comfort when something negative happens, and it helps me feel stronger when I feel like giving up. My faith also has brought me closer to a lot of people through church groups, and those people make my life better.

Anonymous: Not enough. I was raised without religion so I struggle to find a way to work it into my family especially since I have a non-religious husband.

Anonymous: Without the Lord in my life I don't think I would have stayed the course, in my marriage or in my family. Serving the Lord is very important to me. And I want to be a good example to all I meet.

Sylvia: My faith has had high and low spots throughout my life. My belief has never wavered but I have had points in my life where I felt like my faith was the only thing getting me through and other times where my faith was placed solely on my own resources.

Ann, 52: A big impact. Not sure who I would be without my faith. I want people to know that I am a Christian by my actions, not by words.

Anonymous: My higher power gives me the confidence to go after what I want out of life.

Anonymous: Constant struggle

Anonymous: Although I feel like I have lost sight of my religious beliefs a bit as I have grown older, I find that when I do reconnect with God and revel in his presence that it only does me good. Taking the time to thank God for a beautiful day just makes it more beautiful. I am still a woman of faith and that has guided me to be loving, generous, and grateful. I feel like I appreciate life more than if I didn't have my faith.

Kayla, 22: It has kept me centered and also helps relieve stress. Being able to surrender myself to a higher power gives me a sense of peace that is sometimes difficult to obtain. My faith allows me to look at a big picture instead of focusing on problems. I feel like it has also led me to a career that allows me to help others.

Anonymous: Helped me trust that the storm would pass

Anonymous: I know there is something greater than myself and whatever it is guides me daily. Wherever I end my journey will be where I was supposed to end it.

Anonymous: I feel more relaxed and at peace

Anna Grace, 36: My spiritual beliefs have had a HUGE impact on my life. I attended my childhood church well into my 30's. I realized I didn't find out what MY own spiritual beliefs were until I separated myself from that specific church. My family was still there, my childhood was there, my history was there, my dad was pastor there, but I was not there. I got to the point of "I don't believe in much". Once I separated for quite a while, I finally started to see that I have my own beliefs and build on those. Within the last 2-3 years my most spiritual moments have been while meditating, doing yoga or sitting on the side of a mountain. I can't name one or two that occurred within the four walls of a church building. And that is ok!

Anonymous: Faith and spirituality has not been big in my life, and I just try to be kind to people.

Anonymous: I am happier, more content and more in tune with God's will for my life. My walk has become a more permanent fixture in my life. Prayer and worship have become a priority daily.

Dayna, 26: My faith is core to how I operate. My faith guides my head and my heart to make grounded decisions and respond graciously.

Hannah, 18: It has had such a positive impact. My faith and faith community have shown me that I'm not judged on how I look but on the actions I show. That if I do everything I can to give back to God life ends up being pretty great.

Amanda, 29: Not as much as I would like. I would say I have a faith that good things will happen but spiritual beliefs have not played a big role in my life.

Jocelyn: My faith I think plays a big part because I always stride to do the best I can to help out. I think that's what God wants in every one of us. Not all of us will be strong at the same time so we have to help lift each other up so that as a community, we become a strong force. Ultimately, it doesn't matter how much bad you hide, the one that looks at that is God and he's the only one we should try to impress (in my opinion).

Caitlin, 14: My faith has impacted my life greatly! I have been able to really express myself through my faith!

Maddie, 13: My faith and spiritual beliefs has definitely had a big impact on my life because when I didn't go to church as often as I do now, I felt almost as if I was missing something in my life. When I started to go to church I began to feel that missing piece find its way into my lifestyle and because of it, I've met some of my best friends and made new realizations that I wouldn't have been able to make without my beliefs and faith. My lifestyle has changed in ways I wouldn't have seen possible with the way I incorporate my beliefs and faith into my everyday life.

Discussion Questions for All Ages:

Faith is...

_____

_____

_____

_____

_____

_____

Keeping Faith is...

_____

_____

_____

_____

_____

_____

NINE

Trekking on with the Good Life

"The ideals which have lighted my way and time after time have given me new courage to face life cheerfully, have been Kindness, Beauty, and Truth. The trite subjects of human efforts, possessions, outward success, and luxury have always seemed to me contemptible." — Albert Einstein (1879–1955)

Most of the greatest lessons that I have learned in life have come from sharing thoughts and feelings with others. The willingness of women to share their experiences in this workbook is greatly appreciated. My hope is that in each chapter there might be one answer that a woman can relate to, empathize with, and use for her own personal growth.

I know that this idea of loving myself even in my most unlovable moments will be something I continue to work on and strive to achieve. I wish you blessings on your journey, whether that means your faith, your confidence or your trust in yourself and others. I welcome your feedback and invite you to share on the "My Soul Works" Facebook page or go to mysoulworks.com. I know that we learn so much about acceptance when we hear each other's stories.

What was the time in your life that you felt the best about yourself (emotionally, physically, and/or spiritually) and why?

Franki, 37: That question has been stuck in my head since I read it and therefore I am going to answer! It's actually an easy answer for me. It was two years ago. I was absolutely in the best shape physically - I had just finished running my 3rd 1/2 marathon and I set a personal record in it. Three weeks later I did a 150-mile bike ride to raise money and awareness for MS. The ride took place through a beautiful countryside and the scenery took my breath away. On the ride I had a lot of time to think and I did a lot of praying as well. I thanked God for giving me the physical capability to peddle a bike and to be a part of a team that was so compassionately committed to the cause. In those prayers I also let go of some of the struggles I was facing and gave them to God—one of the most important being our years of struggle with infertility. I had accepted that God had a plan for me and that maybe it wasn't to be a mom, and I trusted that plan with my whole heart—even though I didn't know what it was. There was something about those two days of bike riding in the country and prayer that changed me. I felt like my faith and truly been restored and strengthened. I was able to see things differently and was so much more appreciative for my life, my health, my husband and my faith. The following month I learned that I was pregnant and that we were healthy! Since then my faith and love has grown even stronger, and I am so very grateful for every day with my husband, baby girl and I look forward to church every weekend.

Kristy, 38: I felt best about myself once I started teaching and became active in a Methodist Church in Minnesota. Growing up I never felt I was good enough for my peers, or that no matter what I did I would be ostracized for the decisions I made for myself. When I was finally completely on my own and found a group I could actively be part of without question. I finally felt like I could breathe. It was during that time that I met Jeremy and the rest is history. I have no doubt that the struggles I went through growing up helped shape me into who I am today, and as much as I would never want to go through them again, I am glad I had those experiences.

Tracey, 53: 21! Can I go back, please????? Was discovering Catholicism and enjoying the structure and traditions of the Catholic Church, happily in love with a trustworthy man whom I respected, college body--probably the best I ever looked and felt good about. Had almost 3 years of college under my belt and was becoming more interested in the world beyond Wilson. The beginnings of defining who I am--all though in truth I really believe after 40 is when I began to have a good, unapologetic grasp on who Tracey is.

Lisa, 53: Right now! In all aspects! Finally found peace and serenity and acceptance with myself, my son, and everything that has happened in my journey of life! All is good and I thank the Good Lord for sending me on the journey he laid out for me to make me the strong independent loving and successful woman that I am today!

Kyli, 22: Now because I can take a nap & have a Margarita when I want & no little ones to run after…. In honesty though I do think that end of high school and through college is when I did the most growing. You're trying to find out who you want to be in life, what kind of morals you will follow, & how you will get there. I think this time in life is crucial because it's really the only time you're responsible for just yourself & you have to build the strongest version for you for the future!

Brittany, 30: When I gave birth to our baby boy, and my amazing husband was by my side through it all …I was over-joyed and overwhelmed by emotions. I had never felt so blessed and alive!

Anna Grace, 36: For me I'd have to say over the past 3 years, and currently. And why? Because I started putting my-self and my needs first after many years of trying to meet ev-eryone else's needs first. I think it is ironic that I may not be the "best" that I have been physically but I feel the best physi-cally. When I focus on emotions and spirituality I seem to feel great physically. Does that make any sense?

Vickie, 51: I have gradually felt better about myself with every decade. There have definitely been some very hard times along the way, but I've come out stronger after every adversity. I remember being so insecure in my teens and 20's, and I'd be lying if I said I never feel any insecurity now. But I've learned to deal with it better as I age. I also have more resources as I learn more—I take better care of myself physically, mentally, and spiritually. And I've developed stronger and longer friend-ships with time. I would tell my younger self—don't worry, it only gets better!

Frances: When I fell in love again later in life and felt like he saw the "real" me, not just the mom and the wife part of me but the ugly and the beautiful and loved me anyway.

Ashtyn, 28: I would say physically/emotionally I felt the very best about myself at about 17. However, I feel so much closer to God now than I ever have before at 28!

Kristen, 30: I'd say I feel best emotionally and spiritually when I'm taking the best care of myself. This past summer, I focused on running and eating healthy. I spent time with my daughter over summer break, focused on trying to make it to church on Sundays and relaxed. Despite losing a baby during this time, I think I was still in a good place and able to manage difficult emotions because I had a strong foundation.

Jody, 53: When I was pregnant at 35 and 39! Never felt more alive and fulfilled than when I was carrying my beautiful boys!

Barbara: I'd have to agree with 40 onward. Already learned life's lessons the hard way and have been open to what life and God have to bring ever since!

Lisa, 52: In my early 40's, recently divorced, raising two boys and going back to school to change careers. I felt empowered by choices I was making for myself, my children and my future.

Sharon, 51: I have found contentment at many stages of my life for different reasons. In my 20's everything was new— my career, marriage and birth of my children. In my 30's it was raising my children and being a part of their lives. In my 40's it was learning to let them go and watching them become independent. Now in my. 50's it is rediscovering myself as an empty nester. Each stage in my life has been different, but all have been important to help me become the person I am today.

June: I think now, in my 50s. I can see the fruits of my labor in my kids, they are both such wonderful, caring adults. I am satisfied in my job (finally). I care a lot less of what others think of me and I am kinder to myself. I know rushing through life (or each day) is not what I want any more.

Patricia, 65: Throughout my life, every time God presented me with a seemingly insurmountable challenge, I felt best when I exceeded it.

Discussion Question for All Ages:

The best "ME" is...

_____

_____

_____

_____

_____

_____

_____

_____

_____

_____

_____

_____

_____

_____

_____

_____

_____

_____

_____

_____

_____

Author's Notes and Acknowledgments

This book was three years in progress, so many of the answers to questions came from young girls and women who have become high school and college graduates, wives, mothers, grandmothers, and retired women. I cannot thank you all enough for sharing your stories and thoughts with me.

The answers from Sherrie are particularly emotional for me as she lost her battle with cancer on Mother's Day, 2018. I hope that for her amazing daughters and granddaughters, her words will have special meaning. Much love to you all!

I want to make sure to mention the women in my life that have had such a profound influence on me. Starting with my mom Jackie Kelsey, my Godmother, Priscilla Finger, my amazing sisters, Erica and Laura. My nieces, my sister-in-law's, my God sister, pastors, youth, alumni, and extraordinary friends, there are no words to express how much I love all of you!